REVERIES

BOOK I

VINCENT ORION ALÉMAN

WITH ART BY

WILLIAM BLAKE

ATHENA PRESS

Copyright © 2021

Vincent Orion Alémán

Reveries, Book I

With Art by William Blake

www.athenapress.com

ISBN: 978-0-578-92505-9

All rights reserved.

ATHENA PRESS

"Poetry is the spontaneous overflow of powerful feelings: it takes its origin from emotion recollected in tranquility."

—William Wordsworth

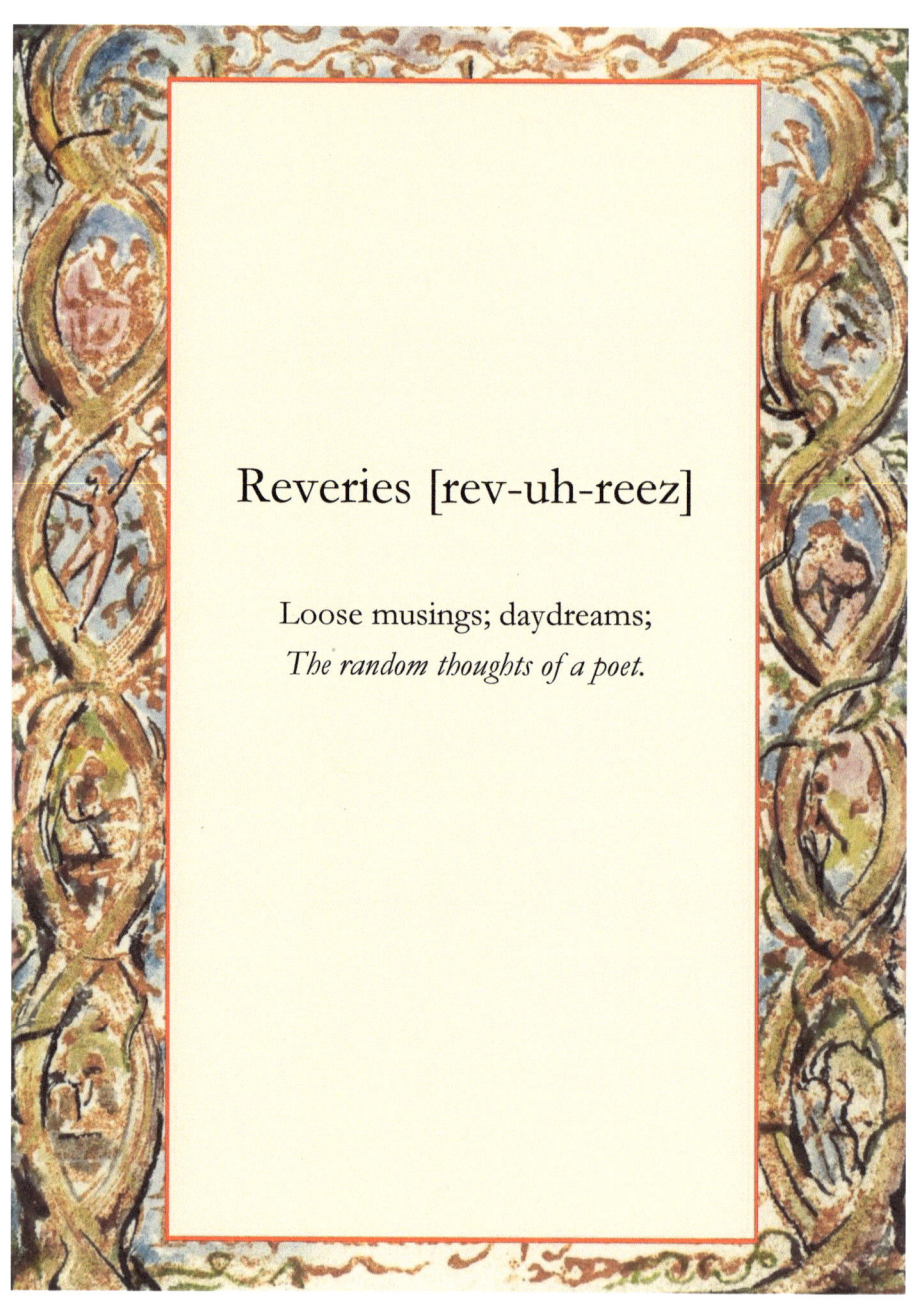

Reveries [rev-uh-reez]

Loose musings; daydreams;
The random thoughts of a poet.

A Sunshine Holiday

LIFE, I WILL MISS YOU

Life, I will miss you.
Feels it was newly issued;
Though thirty years of sparks in my eyes have
    gone by.

Thirty years more, maybe,
Will the sun still enflame me?
Or will ice in my heart leave my
    body bone-dry?

Between now and forever
Is only a short September—
May I see the most while I have the
    light in my eyes;

And love the way I should—
Only being good—
Not causing any other heart to ever cry.

Purity is best for me.
Let me see a world of green.
Banish sleep from my eyes for
    the time flies by.

I pray for length of days
For me and my kids to play;
Eat and drink with my wife always
    in the countryside.

Grant us peace in our nation,
For our temporary station.
May my notebook always be filled
  with these rhymes.

God, be near to me—
Please be pleased!
And every day bring revelations of the
  sublime.

ATHEIST POET

An atheist poet is an oxymoron.
To invoke the Muse is part and parcel of a
 good song.
For every true poet knows that his lines are
 not his,
But he must wait supplicant for inspiring
 bliss.
He is sensitive, for poetry entails detail;
And no one can live sensitively and unwell.
And it is nearest the Divine that we are most
 good.
The ancient bards were called "Holy";
 this was understood.
God's peculiar care is fashioned with all
 accoutrements,
Complete with fine lines and musical
 instruments.
It is no shock that in our age the poet is rare,
For if true beauty can't be found in God,
 then where?

My heart bleeds—
    So much to say.
The poet the world needs
    Is still M.I.A.
Religion, stacked on Philo-
    Sophy, with a tongue o'
        Liquid gold.
Only a drip falls from the manifold!
More study, more sturdy
    The pen must be;
Cut out my organs and play on
    minor keys—
Lyric Poems—so my people have
    something to read;
Shake the world's foundation—
    Let them see a pure breed.

THE POET'S CUE

What is the poet's cue?
When the arrow shoots through
    His gallbladder.
Nothing else will do.
    Nothing else matters

But our own common clay—
The unacknowledged legislators
    of the world
Play on strings what all hearts
    long to say.

A sacerdotal ministry.
    And just like Levi
Was apportioned land and tithes,
    The poet too meeds royalty.

Divine, beside the farmer—
    So they often conjoin;
Both giving life its substance
    Erelong we disjoint.

FOR HIS AGE

The poet dies with his age
   And his language.
Those who would translate his page
   Do him damage.
It is for such a time as this
   you have been called to the stage.
Two generations from now
   you're a bore, not a sage.

BOTH AND EITHER

There were two brothers:
Both and Either.
Either was Both
And Both was Neither.
For Both pleased all,
Which pleased nobody;
While Either had both
Enemies and buddies.

CINDERELLA

You can go to the royal ball,
Pull up in a magical
Pumpkin-carriage lead along
By mice transformed to stallions.
But you must be home by midnight.
Did Cinderella put up a fight?
Like the guests of *this* wonderland
Who transgress every rule in sight?

FOOLS

You break my heart;
    rip it apart.
I wish you were smart;
        but now it just smarts.
Were you deceived? It's hard to believe
That you conceived such vulgarities.
Or is it some sort of mental disorder
Passed on from your father or mother,
Who didn't care, sent you anywhere,
So that an education was rare?
Joined idiots are more serious—
Now confidence mixes with prejudice;
Commonsense preachers seem invidious:
"Don't tell me my world is illegitimate!"
You talk too fast, or too slow;
You're an imbecile, don't you know?
Although you may have never been told,
Read it on your own in the Bible:
"Seek wisdom"; "Be prudent";
"He who hates correction's stupid".
"A lazy hand is a disgraceful son"—
All you ever want to do is have fun.
"Discretion will protect you"—
You ladies will soon have a baby in the
    womb.
Your grandiosity exceeds all bounds;
The comedy leads to bonds or to the
    ground.

Two classes Solomon puts forth:
The wise and the foolish of all the earth.
The first are the few; the latter, the many.
The first live on books and love to study.
They wish to see the world a better place,
But their progress is by the fools erased.
Oh, Jerusalem, Jerusalem!
How I've longed to gather you like a hen
Gathers her chicklings
    Under her wings,
        Yet you were not willing.

AMBITION

Stupidity leads the ambitious astray
After strange women, riches and fame.
Lacking spiritual content, they're discontent—
Whom Aristotle styles "the incontinent"—
And grasping to fill up the void within;
While all substance is but a shadow dim:
A parable of virtue divine—
Patience, love, peace of mind;
Chiefly confidence—which can't be bought,
But are only spoils of hard battles fought.
No fist-fight makes masculinity;
No fling confers sexuality.
Loving the truth and bearing your cross
Through the onslaught burns off the dross.
Glory is not a gas that you can pass,
But the smoke of a sacrifice reduced to ash.
Great exploits are not man-made,
But mandated on high through gifts inlaid.
Most assuredly great men seek great things,
But their activities are free of vanities.
Do your job well and do not weary
Yourself with wealth; let God choose your salary.
Invest in your soul and you'll never go alone,
While avarice never finds its way home.

OL' BEN FRANK

Ol' Ben Frank retired at forty-five.
The Bloods and the Crips expire by forty-fives.
We all want to be kings, unhindered in our desires.
And unless we inherit a fortune from our sires,
We can come about it through diligence and due time;
Or through crime, plunder, violence and rapine.
Rabid canines are shackled in chains and shot dead;
Law-abiding citizens are privileged to keep their head.
What separates men from the beasts is one thing:
    Reason;
To dwell among men one must abstain from treason.
Throw Daniel's enemies into the lion's den,
They'll perish; but how is it lions don't rule men?
Our thoughts are our fangs; our wisdom our claws;
Superior to brute strength are all the laws.
Ben Franklin built on the foundation of his genius,
Putting all the money he ever got into his reading.
The riches of wisdom transmuted into gold;
Although he had to wait until he was a little old.
But then he was free to make your bifocals,
Play with electricity, and travel the globe—
Instead of being locked up in an institution.
Salute Ben Frank for signing the constitution!
You confess him the better man when you do ill
For money and find his face on the hundred dollar bill.

"Tricks and treachery are the practice of fools,
that don't have brains enough to be honest."
—Benjamin Franklin

STILL GOING

I was born in Miami—
In Jackson Memorial Hospital;
Raised on the Beach,
Where no one is hospitable.
We call it the "Dirty South"—
I rocked dirty dreadlocks
To my chest, tank-tops,
Dickies and Reeboks.
Mixing white with my green,
Sniffing to get up to speed;
Ringing up your groceries
As my nose starts to bleed.
Masked up in a bush,
Lying in ambush,
To hijack an Escalade,
Leave it in the Everglades.
Everywhere that I go
My machete goes too.
This chico is loco—
Will chop off your coco;
Like the "Chopper"—a.k.a.
The AK-47—
Got my friend a life-sentence
And someone a trip to Heaven.
I was going down fast
And just about to crash
When at age sixteen
The Lord caught me in His grasp.
This is my survival story.
If you think my rhymes are corny
You don't know how far I've come
Or where I'm still going.

POSEIDON

I see you, Poseidon,
    With your trident:
The chariot you ride in
    Is pulled by dolphins
And encircled by sea-nymphs.
The party looks quite lively
    As you dive deep
To the bottom of the sea,
Where stands your castle
    And a perpetual feast.
But I smell you—you're briny;
Your seaweed is slimy;
And is that I see beside thee
Your lover boy's hiney?
You are unstable as the waves:
No calm, now in a craze;
Infertile to our seeds.
Avaunt! you and your steeds.

DEBAUCHERY

Debauchery
Is not all it's chalked up to be.
Better call it *an achy head*
And *stupidity*.
Or worse yet, It can mean
The total loss of dignity.
So philosophers brought their young disciples to see
The Bacchanalian orgy—
A drunken frenzy:
To give 'em the fear of God
And of partying too hard.
But once in a while Dionysus may be called for—
If just to remind us not to hanker for more.

    So if you must be a heathen,
Do it in such a way you would make it to Heaven—
    The best of both worlds.
              Youth is on the wing!
That doesn't mean a fling—
Like a Persian king
Would dismiss the queen
To revel in his wine
And debauch the concubines—
The one's who like it rough
And can take a good rebuff.
Your woman is game enough
To put up with all that stuff.
She would even call your bluff.
If you only knew your luck!

TEMPTATION

Temptation is that which feels better than what you have
But resolves in dissolution, and the option for you to grab,
Or to decline in hopes of the Lord giving you something more
Than you ever could have imagined was in store.
I know the true way when it smells of sacrifice,
For who could ever live with the Lord and not pay a price?
These are tricks, these are treats in the center of the Garden,
To see who inherits the blessing and God's pardon.

"We should strain every nerve to avoid wickedness."
—Aristotle

Satan Watching the Endearments of Adam and Eve

THE FORCE OF LOVE

Sex is a powerful thing, meant to unify
A husband and wife, so they can multiply
In family—the bedrock of society,
Cities and nations; and so spreads God's decree.
To be unequally yoked is a singular tragedy.
But the force of love has such a binding property,
It can leave a woman knocked up, far out to sea,
Addicted to a man she doesn't really care to see;
Till another snatch her up, enraptured under the spell.
But for all this love making, it's perpetual Hell.
For a match made in Heaven, let Heaven intervene.
Wait your turn, lest you be caught off guard downstream.
When kindred spirits are kindled by love's flame,
The two become one, they are never the same.
They make their own society, they're never alone.
It's the only way that a house can become home.

The Whirlwind of Lovers, for Dante's Inferno

RAMÓN LULL

Ramón Lull
Knew how a girl to pull;
In the old days when Spain
Was still under the Pope's rule.
But some one señorita
Made him a raging bull.
Next to her all were dull;
She had her home in his skull.
But she was a wedded wife
With a lively family life
And knew nothing of Ramón's
Continual inner strife.
"May the best man win!
Fie! on manmade tradition.
Love is a greater law
Than anyone has given."
So resolved the young hidalgo
Who soon made his love known;
And with every declination
He pursued her more and more;
Till she was his, all alone,
Begging the question, "Why,
Ruin my life?" And with a sigh
He replies, "You've ruined mine".
She unbosoms her silk blouse
At the desperate man's answer,
And he finds her young breasts
Eaten away with cancer.
So shocked! he staggered back,
Far back, to the monastery,
And swore his life to theology
And to never marry.

UTOPIA

If you see a fool,
    Down and out,
Do you give him a hand
    Or a kick in the mouth?
Milk him for all he's got left—
    Is this your right?
It seems to me love would produce
    A happier plight.
With all the money in the world
    The rich keep getting richer:
Evenly squeezing the little man
    Out of the picture.
When you could educate! elevate!
    Your praise would be endless!
But you hold back Utopia
    By your injustice.

"Our society is run by insane people for insane objectives,
and I think I'm liable to be put away as insane for expressing that.
That's what's insane about it."
—John Lennon

VENUS VS. PLUTO

Venus is Beauty,
Family and Duty,
Country, Modesty,
Summed up in Piety—
Or "Pietas", coined the Romans.
But these modern foemen
Worship Pluto—although Saturn
Forms their subject matter:
The gloomy reign of Hades
Where Satan has his shadow
In the far recesses
    Of the no tomorrow;
Where darkness has a face,
    And it's wholly ugly:
Sexual slavery;
Abusive tyranny;
Pain stacked on top of pain;
Low degradation and shame.
There's Death, Idolatry;
No hope of liberty.
Knife slash and blood splash,
And every disgusting thing
    You can think—
Like a serpent
    Coiling until you're spent.
Beware your footstep
And that which follows up
The Mount Delectable
Or down to hollow stuff.
But at the entrance of Hell
I saw the inscription,
Not the one of Dante,
But of "Communism".

10,000 CE

By the year 5,000 CE
Humans had successfully
    Digitized the psyche,
So that they practically
    Have life eternally—
Through a biomedically
    Engineered body;
And when these are done
They get transferred to new ones.
Life was all a bunch of fun
Amongst the world's top 1%—
The only survivors of Armageddon.
The population
Is a fixed five hundred million...

They do not have children—
Their bodies are sterile,
Having exchanged that burden
For a constant revel.
They've all quit their day-jobs!
Every basic need
Was handled by robots.
But as they fed their greed,
For centuries and centuries
They started to change.
By 10,000 CE
Their minds were deranged.
Their arm hair grows to feathers,
Their nails are talons—
Immortal Nebuchadnezzars,
Whore of Babylon.

PROMETHEUS TO ZEUS

You are the boss;
    You hold it down,
        Exuding your energy.
Let all toss
    Down their crowns
        For Zeus the Almighty.
None could ever contradict you—
So you stole Europe away,
And turned IO to a heifer
And left her that way to stay!
Such insolence reeks of the menace—
Tho I know you're wont to say,
"Greatness can have no limits,
But it sets the rules to play.
It is survival of the fittest—
The race would fall into decay
Without a god to snatch his wishes.
Who needs humans anyway?
They serve me, not me them;
And it is a mercy shown
When I rule them from Heaven
And take their tribute that I own!"
'Tis true, 'tis true, Lord Zeus,
We confess you are thrice blessed.
But can we not come to a truce?
Leave them their own women at least.
You scoff now, hardy and loud
And turn your back on the crowd.
But what's this? I've got your torch!
Leaping from Olympus' porch.
Go now, man! and take this
When someone bigger would do you harm.
You need not fear a lightning fist
Once you have donned a *firearm*.

MORAL

Brawn oft lacks intelligence.
Necessity breeds invention;
Weakness needs self-defense:
Arts, science, laws and convention.
But these are just such battlements
As leave shafts rankling in the breast.
It is on account of this
That mankind dominates the beasts.
And so these two go side by side:
Natural beauty, force and rule,
And the outcasts who can't abide,
If not by sharpening their tools.

The Assassination of Julius Caesar

Tyrants beware:
Where there are slaves
    there is fear.
All empires recycle
When conquerors grow fickle
On the fat of their substance,
And the hungry want in.
Replace man with A.I.,
By robots you'll still die.

ICING ON THE CAKE

Anything past thirty is icing on the cake.
The twenties are when we see the best God makes—
Whether soldiery or poetry. The daemon leaves off
At the first disturbances of a catarrhal cough.
The demi-gods start to lose battles afield—
Still hungry for victory, yet forced to yield.
Many species expire at the time of procreation;
And every thirty years arises a generation.
Think how many friends at that age are still here...
So many die in so many ways every year.
If we haven't drunken deep by then, it's our fault;
And scarcely will putting off ever put a halt
To self-induced ignorance. And why fear so to die?
It is our duty. In war it is cowardice to fly.
If ever a Roman soldier abandoned his station,
He with a tenth of his legion faced decimation.
That's how they took the world; and nothing leads to
    slavery
Like when those who should be brave start wavering.
Kill us all past thirty for the sake of the teens!
The time of team sports, young love and pipe dreams.
The Viking men bewailed a natural death,
And if they 'scaped the battle unscathed they slashed
    their own flesh,
So at least they could die with some type of war scars.
We're content to go nowhere, if just we go far.

INTOLERANCE

I'm intolerant of you?
You're intolerant of me!
I try to live by the motto:
 "Be and let be".
Make your impact on the world
 while I make mine.
We'll see who's the heavy-
 weight champ in due time.
But you sneak in the laws
And fine-print your clause.
The multitudes can be duped
 to follow any cause.
You ask for a hug
And squeeze till it throbs,
With the arms of that many-
 headed monster—
A mob.

MEN WITHOUT CHESTS

Men without chests—
This is the agenda.
Remove manhood from the breast,
You have a perfect surrender;
As the mutants acquiesce
To all of your plan.
Read C.S. Lewis's
The Abolition of Man

SUN & MOON

The heart is the sun,
The brain is the moon.
Monday follows on Sunday
And so too
The passions keep raging
With nothing to check them
But the faint and pallid light
Of reflection.
The moon moves the waves,
And makes lunatics:
Too much thought or too little,
Both make sick.
Twelve hours of the day
Are dedicated each,
So that our integrity
Won't suffer a breach.

MAN IS NOT YET FULLY MAN

Man is not yet fully man
Until he does the best he can:
Polished and civil, attentive,
Intelligent, self-possessive;
Master of Language, and Learning,
Emotion, Health, Finance, Hygiene.
Till then he is an apish man.
Try to live up the best you can.

WASHINGTON

In that intermediary state
    between life and sleep,
There rode up one of regal bearing
    on a gallant steed.
He was recognized at once
    as our general in war;
But I saw in that personage
    that there was so much more.

CONVO VS. TECHNO

During the Renaissance
    Manly recreation
Involved the sciences
    And enlightened conversation.
It was a pastime
    To prattle over a mug of ale
On Classics, the sublime,
    And what made the world well.
This was at once more entertaining
    And more beneficial.
Nothing like social-media
    To make anti-social.
Skull-caps flap in the wind,
    They're so empty—
When all we need for a good time
    Is to be smart and friendly.

CURIOSITY

Follow Curiosity wherever she goes.
She'll mess you up bad,
    keep you on your toes—
When you come to learn
    what nobody else knows...
Oh snap! But you can't say that life blows.
It's better to know the truth
    than to be in the dark,
Like darkness is inferior to a candle spark.
Here is safety, God's face,
    and a cup overflowing—
When you come to know the thoughts
    that God's knowing.

THE UNMOVED MOVER

The definition of *Good*
    is to be good at something.
In other words,
    something must come before nothing.
Because *negative* is simply deficit of what is:
It does not exist
    except for some point of reference.
All of Space and Time
    must be preceded by Matter;
For what is *Space between objects*
    or *Time-Travel*
Without objects,
    the distances of which to measure?
And can nothing produce ex-nihilo
    at pleasure?
The good is what is,
    and what always has been,
Going hand in hand with a good creation.
Why glorify darkness?
    Next to the light it's over.
It all fades or goes back
    to The Unmoved Mover.

THE INEFFABLE NAME

El, Anu, or Yahweh—
Which one is it? None can say.
Father to the fatherless,
Or "Large-Breasted" El-Shaddai?
Paul calls upon Theos
Which is a derivative of Zeus.
The word "God" is Old Germanic
Meaning *libations of juice*.
And why not? He is true wine,
The Bread of Life, The Living Vine,
Rose of the Valley, Rock of Ages,
Morning Star—all things divine!
Multitudinous, He breaks out
In sundry personalities:
The blood-red Mars of war;
Bright Venus, goddess of beauty.
You can clip off Cupid's wings;
He will be back as Valentines.
Tell Bacchus that he drinks too much,
And St. Patrick will spike your punch.
In Him we live and move and breathe
So that some worship *Everything*;
But it would be a tragedy
Failing to know this sentient Being.

MANDALA

Who are you?
Why are you? Why are we?
I don't believe in a hereafter,
    Why should I believe
        In your goodness?
What is goodness?
Am I lying to myself?
Is God schizophrenic?
Maybe it's all relative.

But then why do you force me one way?
Why do you curse those gone astray?

Maybe everything is based on love
    And you lead
        As you please;
Not strictly on "virtue",
    But on love:
And you love those who love you,
    Permitting certain harmless deviations.

Maybe you are not "good",
    But you are love.
Maybe good is you,
    As you choose,
        And never a set of rules.
Maybe sometimes love is what we consider evil,
    In order to work out love:
        Unpredictable;
        Not necessarily "good",
        But perfectly balanced;
        Round Mandela:
        Love is wholesome.

BEAUTY IS MORALITY

Beauty is morality—
    Or better yet, vice versa.
You can't escape this reality
    Though you force a
Pretty show. Bad can never be
    beautiful.
But this is where the definition of
    terms plays a role.
Each thing has its particular faculty:
    The body may be fair,
    The mind be most ugly.
We must see past the admixture
    and properly dissect,
Until each area blooms in its own
    respect.

BEAUTY IS ART

Beauty is art
And art is effort.
When I see the fine lines
On some antique treasure
Designed with a mind
To produce pleasure,
The artist transcends time—
Love lives forever.

When I see the beautiful
In nature around me—
As the flowers are growing
And the birds are sounding—
Do I fail to behold
The travail of a thousand
Lives striving to be whole
Before they lie grounding?

Blood, sweat and tears
Make a thing worth observing.
Is it an accident of the years
That lovers keep serving?
That the species keep evolving,
And the world keeps turning?
There is an artist here—
The best of all, the most concerning.

HOW HE LEADS ME

I know who He is by how He leads me:
No blessings come into my hands
    to make me greedy;
But they are one for all, all for one.
I feel Him reaching
    For the soul too far gone,
        Till I start weeping,
            And preaching!
He's leading me the right way
    and I know it,
Although the majority are not for it.
An oasis in the wilderness;
A lamp in the darkness;
A hive and honeycomb in the belly of a
    carcass.

"And Moses said unto the Lord...
Show me your ways, that I may know you."
Exodus 33:12-13

I'M A BABYLONIAN

I'm a Babylonian—
    Not the kind that buried
Enemies up to their necks
    In a desert cemetery;
Covered their heads with honey,
    Left them to fire-ants;
Cut out their tongue
So that they couldn't rave and rant.
Not that kind,
    But kind of like Niram Sin—
The Mesopotamian
    Who taught the life-lesson
Through tales of failed tyrants
    And selfish-ambition:
"Do your duty
    In the embrace of your woman."

DID GOD CREATE THE WHOLE WORLD FOR LOVERS?

Did God create the whole world
    for lovers—
        like you and me?
Is the story of all history
    our story?
Are we the beginning and the end?
    Though so many miss out.
Are we His holy experiment
    that just can't go south?
A modest man, woman and home
    in the country scenery,
Each one with an eye to the other,
    singly;
Talking, laughing, loving, learning,
    working hard at what we love.
I wouldn't trade Heaven on Earth
    for a Heaven above.

Beatrice Addressing Dante

HOME

We all start in a home—
    Be it a homeless shelter;
With someone to call our own—
    Be it a neglecter.
The image is there, the human archetype:
The standard is a mother who loves her children right.
Add a father, it's complete. Old Laertes' son
Boasted against the Cyclops His lineage run.
We're not beasts, eating raw flesh—
    We have a human soul
That needs another, a soul-mate
    to love and hold.
The dream is a home, with a happy wife and tots.
And if you've picked the right one then you've hit the jackpot!
Once you've been through so much, and your souls are knit,
Nothing can match it! Throw in Wagner's Ring with it.
Family is my religion, if anyone asks.
I've got shotguns and long-sword for those who trespass.
We pledge allegiance in this land to the flag of Alémán.
Keep your nightclubs, STDs and condoms.
I grow gardens! I've got goats and chickens.
Go conquer the world, while I conquer these dishes.
I love playing with my kids, and cooking a meal:
Nobody like them knows what I feel.
I've come a long way, but ever since I was ten
I was a smart boy who worshipped women.
But I knew deep inside I was looking for one.
Deeper down inside I was looking for home.

STILL FRAMES

Reading is a languid pleasure.
But when the still frames
 reel out in conversation,
No movie is ever better!

And conversation is boring.
Unless it is with my wife
Who speaks on life
With such vigor as can leave
 nobody snoring.

HORACE

I was not, like you, trained in the harsh
    school of war.
At the age you donned the toga
    I was little more than a bore.
But ever since then, it is my belief,
    I was led
Through a school of philosophy deeper
    than that in which you were bred.
To doodle down these ditties has been
    my childhood pastime.
You've got a vast volume, with more
    chapters than mine.
Though I love and emulate you,
    you often lead astray—
So I pray, "Beloved of the Muses",
    to be the mouthpiece of Yahweh.

FAME IS THE GIANT'S SHADOW

Fame is the Giant's shadow
That naturally follows.
He does not seek it,
    but it comes
For what he has done
In seeking to fulfill duty—
Being really and truly,
God manifest on Earth
Doing His own work.

WORDSWORTH

When I go off into nature
   I take Wordsworth with me.
The book stays at home;
   his ghost is in my memory.
      Show me the Evergreens!
Far better still
   is a bright day in May,
For me to climb up some craggy hill
   To a high place and survey
      The vast horizon!
Undaunted, upheld by Atlas' might.
It almost reminds me of the ocean
   skyline reaching out of sight,
Way back home in Southern Florida.
   I'll not speak on it too much;
For it takes the Smokey Mountains
   to outweigh the water's touch.

HUMIDITY

I love to sweat—
Humid in my blood.
The Spaniard's bayonet
Would still crusade through
      floods
Of gore up to the hilt—
So runs the medieval lore.
Melancholera is spilt
On our curls, eyes, and more.
The rolling tongue signifyeth
A boulder rolling o'er,
That doesn't stop until it dyeth
(Tho for love it's most sore).
What is this land, what of this
      climate?
So cold and frigid is the air;
How stiff—unlike an island:
Humid, dripping everywhere.

THE LAZY LITERATE

Damn you Tacitus!
Damn you Shui Hu Zhuan!
And all the rest on my reading
    list—
Your volumes are too long!
I'd love to sit at your feet
Nourishing on celestial bread.
But the time is fleeting—
I'd rather talk with my wife
    instead.
I will be back for ammunition,
To give her a good impression:
What is life without good sex
And good conversation?
But I'll miss you, role models;
Still pick you up and fondle.
Though it's doubtful I'll ever
Read you cover to cover.

MEMORY

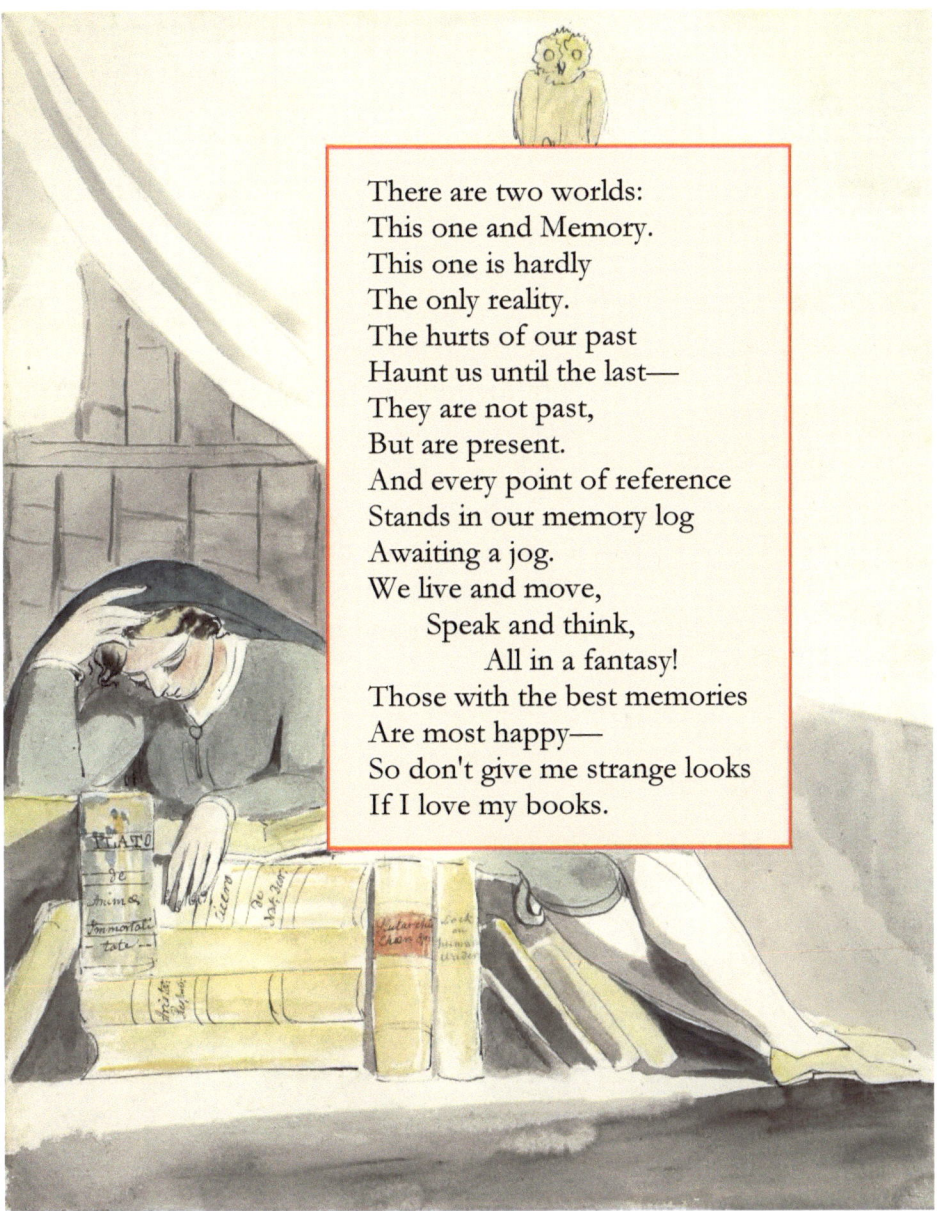

There are two worlds:
This one and Memory.
This one is hardly
The only reality.
The hurts of our past
Haunt us until the last—
They are not past,
But are present.
And every point of reference
Stands in our memory log
Awaiting a jog.
We live and move,
    Speak and think,
        All in a fantasy!
Those with the best memories
Are most happy—
So don't give me strange looks
If I love my books.

MYTHOLOGY

It is the archetypes I need,
Not the flowery language.
I can fill the gaps myself;
Give me action on the pages.
But where this is wanting
Dialogue turns a demagogue.
All the content has been lodged
With Homer and Hesiod.

The boisterous spirit of Ulysses
Breathed life into Attica.
Prudent and adventurous
Proved the great men of that era.
Witty sayings; large conquests;
Epitome of manliness.
But something more than just mere man
Is needed if we would find rest.
Out of Palestine alone arose
The flower of paradise.
Greek is funner to peruse;
Hebrew is Lashon Hakodesh.
Looking my daughters in the face
The Scriptures outweigh all of them;
And I question, What has Athens
To do with Jerusalem?

"If I forget thee, O Jerusalem,
let my right hand forget her cunning."
Psalm 137:5

HE IS GRACIOUS

"He is gracious, this I know",
I will tell myself again;
For experience has shown
Time and time that He's my friend.
I know not what will befall
These ten thousand by my side,
But I hear the Lord's call
And in Him I will abide.
I believe no longer
That He's breathing down my neck,
Like a jealous warmonger,
But He shows me due respect.
He is kind, near and loving,
Often speaking openly.
Or is all this mercy now
For all the times He's broken me?

DAILY BREAD

Our Father, give us this day our daily bread.
It is for this purpose I've risen from bed—
To find a strong inoculating antidote for my head.
Books open, knees bent, and the page is reread.
I need a heavy dose of Seneca and some Plutarch.
The sun is just coming up, but my soul is too dark.
Wonderful Counselor, after a bout of meditation,
My worries are allayed, my anger is abated.
I've taken some notes on how to be a better man;
Help me to apply them the best that I can,
Till tomorrow my notepad I pray you will fill.
It is a sign of getting well when we know we are ill.
May the metamorphosis that I've started go on.
Sure I've made some progress, but I'm so far from done.
Let the strong spell of philosophy enchant,
And your Spirit influence, till these lies I recant.

Laocoön

VERY BROKEN

Some things will never change.
Some scars can derange.
Like rejection, worthlessness—
The root of all baseness;
The spring of ever needing to prove
Oneself deserving of some love.
All the other kids play so well
While I'm living Hell in a cell.
If only I was adopted
And had a giant's confidence,
I would kick the ball so hard
It would fly over the fence.
But here I'm limping, trying to believe
I am somebody,
And I shun the mirror when my scars
    tell me
That I'm ugly.

Pity

IDENTITY

Man's most primitive inclination is for life.

All life comes from some source.

We all cater to the sources we believe have the most enduring life, in hopes that they will give us life.

This *catering* is *obeying*, and this *imparting of life* is *loving*.

To look at it another way, we do not simply cater to or obey, but we mimic, in hopes of enduring like that which we mimic.

All power-sources exert themselves. This is *emanation*. But on their outermost extremities they must take on some frame or form. Spirit is life, power, energy, raw essence; but spirit first appears in the lower forms of words, images, ideas, Logos; (*lower* in that much is lost in translation, as in translating a feeling into a word—*love* into *I love you*). These forms come to us as vessels, and by obeying or mimicking, adding faith or confidence, we imbibe waters of life.

We all seek identity, life, love, strength, stability, endurability from some *thing*—and that *thing* we worship as *Father*.

All of our hopes, identities, and strengths are built on faulty foundations: Everything is mutable and passing.

We are all weak. Even the strong are weak; although they are less likely to know it.

Those who feel most the vanity of their own existence—those who know themselves—are most intelligent and most willing to seek a better life. In this way weakness can become an advantage.

To encounter God is to feel at once both one's own inferiority and the strongest source. The greater the encounter (which may be aided by one's innate humility), the greater the impression.

Profoundly moved thus, *anyone* will obey in everything, becoming more than a mere man...

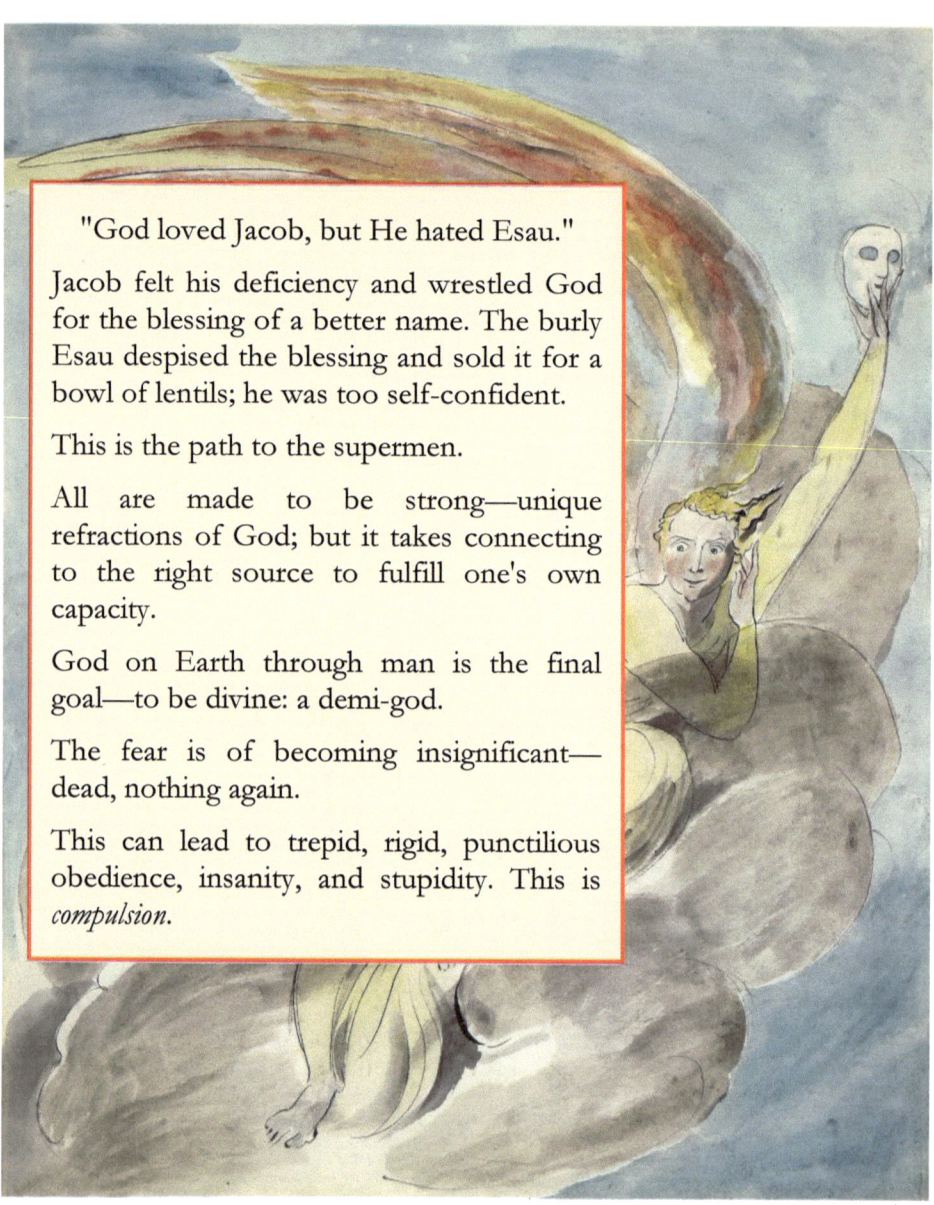

"God loved Jacob, but He hated Esau."

Jacob felt his deficiency and wrestled God for the blessing of a better name. The burly Esau despised the blessing and sold it for a bowl of lentils; he was too self-confident.

This is the path to the supermen.

All are made to be strong—unique refractions of God; but it takes connecting to the right source to fulfill one's own capacity.

God on Earth through man is the final goal—to be divine: a demi-god.

The fear is of becoming insignificant—dead, nothing again.

This can lead to trepid, rigid, punctilious obedience, insanity, and stupidity. This is *compulsion*.

But there is a place of *paternity*; a filial spirit which grows from a long relationship with the Father. Here obedience is second nature, as when a child lives out the nature of his father; not like the obedience of a slave obeying strange commands. Here divergences are not met with such fear of falling from grace, but they are seen as small lapses which are covered by grace. This was the plan all along—the Gospel of David:

Legitimacy. Sonship. A heavenly identity.
Adoption. Belonging.
Never feeling worthless again.

The best way out of *compulsion* and into *sonship* is by acting like a son: that is, by simply doing what you know you should do; *being yourself*, trusting that you are good like your Father; and trusting that He is just and will not hurt you for trifles. Overall it is by confessing that you have a good Father. Believing in grace is the highest praise! Not abusing grace, but living by it and in it.

VANILLA-EXTRACT

My boy loves vanilla-
Extract—it's a killa.
Tastes like hard liquor.
He asked for a "sippa".
With a dab in the cap,
He threw his head back,
Choked and scrubbed off his black
Tongue with the kitchen rag.
I said, *What's the fuss?*
And like a genius
Drank him under the table
Till I huffed and puffed.
Gave my wife a big kiss,
When one of my guests
Kindly taught me this:
One of the ingredients
In vanilla-extract is
Beaver anal-gland drip...
I smiled big and added,
"That's why we eat organic."

STAINED GLASS

Dreadlocks and ganja;
Prayer-poses and mantras;
Flamboyant embroidered robes;
Temples of monolithic stones;
Dresses and Sari-scarfs;
Face-paint and body-art;
Self-respecting modesty,
Reflection of divinity;
Temple bells and incense;
Altars and elephants;
Lotuses and jewelry;
Murals and statuary.
It all crosses me as odd—
These gifts of the blue god.
Would it be too much to ask—
Can we get some stained glass?

"I am convinced that everything has come down to us from the banks of the Ganges."
—Voltaire

RIDE, SI SAPIS

When seriousness
    becomes a chronic disease,
It's time to lighten up
    and light up some trees.
If you're wise then be happy—
    for what else are we here?
A stern face and low spirits
    only shorten the years.

Mirth

THE FAIRY EATER

As my children and I
Sit Indian style
On our living room rug
And the rays from the sun
Descending in the west
Shoot in through the glass
Emblazoning our face
We stare off into space
At the motes dancing free
And pretend they're fairies.

"So what do they say?",
I ask them in play.
"They seem to be saying,
'Take me ice-skating!'",
My eldest girl cries.
Her sister espies
With oracular art,
"Give your family your heart!"
We cannot pinch one!
They startle and dart.
My boy resorts to eating them
Like a shark.

AMBULANCE

Working on the ambulance
I so happened to chance
Upon a man with nose cancer.
I loaded him on my stretcher,
And face-to-face I saw the crater
That ate away like a canker
Through all the surrounding bone
Where his nose was now gone—
Black and bloody, fresh and runny.
I thought, "Who can love this man?"
Sometimes I ask that of myself
And think that my wife can.
For as I wheeled him out the room
A pretty young lady
Would not stop kissing his wound
And saying, "I love you, baby."

JUST SCALES

While the emperor has naked "minnows"
    swimming between his legs,
The Roman frontier infantry
    is draining down the dregs.
Pleasure and pain
    both have an equal measure—
Put the weight on one end
    it goes up on the other.
Infinite decadence has no place,
    like all pain:
Like an all-golden face
    would be an effeminate bane
        only suited to complain.
Hardiness comes from hardship;
And often it is a kindness
    when Fortune gives us the slip.

TV

Thou shall not make for thyself
 A graven image
To bow down before it
 And pay it homage;
Not of wood, stone,
 Precious metal
  Or even *plastic*,
On an altar, or a wall,
 To stare at it,
  Like an addict.

FRENCH WINE

Why is French wine
So much better than mine?
Is it cultured, like the French—
Despite some decadence?
For millennia now
   they have tilled the same soil.
But America is new,
   and like a child it's still spoiled.

MODESTY

"The naked woman's body is a portion of eternity
too great for the eye of man."
—William Blake

When a woman's fully naked
    she's all that.
No further adornment is needed
    but that back.
Cover it up for all of that!
    This is a prideful show.
Modesty can go places
    Beauty can't go.
To hide your wealth is not shame
    but decency—
Being kind to your kind brothers
    in need.
Save those gems for your king—
    if you get my drift—
Not for drifters; your treasures
    should be a gift.

TRAIN STATION
(A DREAM)

Everything is cloudy,
Everything is grey;
Like a black and white movie
On an overcast day.
Walking through a train station,
I can hardly lift my eyes.
But one grabs my attention:
The conductor walking by.
He has a long black mustachio
That curls up at the ends;
His face seems to glow,
He enjoys how it bends.
I trace 'round one of the circles—
It seems to never stop—
Like a hypnotic spiral,
Till I reach the tip-top.
And at that very place
The point lands on his cheek
Color starts to fill his face
Like a watercolor leak.
And so spreads part by part
The whole canvas of my heart—
An innocent private pleasure
Brings color to the dark.

The Young Poet's Dream

TEXT MESSAGES

Carelessness in writing
    Becomes careless manners.
Use your apostrophes,
    Semicolons
        And polished grammar.
It's a representation of you,
    And you must be excellent.
Think you're writing letters,
    Not just text messages.

ERROR

I believe homosexuality
   is an error,
Because for me to go near poop
   is a terror;
And something so much prettier
   gives birth to all things;
Errors don't add up.
     It doesn't have Nature's ring.

RESEARCH

There's a secret that I know,
But nobody taught it me.
You must find out on your own
If you would be truly free.
For if you don't have what it takes
To unlock the code,
You'll have nothing to fall back on
When your world explodes.

NEWTON

Love breeds genius:
Curiosity, in all its ways—
Heightened consciousness,
Surveying creation's vast array.
With flaws it must contend;
The rules it cannot bend;
Steadfast until the end,
Content to be condemned.
But the analytic mind
Soon begins to unwind—
Swallowed up by the abyss,
Seeking details in mist.
Finding the human heart—
That formidable foe—
The lobes of the brain split apart
And all is woe.
Some knowledge we should let over-
    reach us,
Lest in seeking too much we end up
    like Nietzsche.
Even Newton, after his lapse of sanity,
Rebounded to a more normal humanity.

Newton at the Bottom of the Sea

The Soul Exploring the Recesses of the Grave

WHERE SHALL I GO?

Lord, if I go
To where shall it be?
    Will the fabric of the cosmos
    Lift like a blindfold
    So I can fully know
What goes on behind the scenes,
With ancestral spirits—
A new angelic being?

Or did the ghosts come first
    And then the race of men?
So I'll put on a new corpse
    Once again
        Intermeshed,
    Losing my divine sense
    Until the time I repent
And get back on course.
One thing is for sure...

I can't live without You.
Maybe there's a perfect city
 with no scoundrels:
  White robes
   Talkin' Cicero;
    Walkin' about ivory columns
     in the style of Rome;
Meet and greet—
The brethren welcome you home!

...

A Family Reuniting in Heaven

Maybe not.
Maybe we rot
    And fertilize the soil,
And up springs
Another who sings
    Your praises while they toil.

NOAH

One, two, or three
In Noah's boat on the sea.
What is Earth? Just a pea.
Did He make it all for me?
If many nations drown and sink,
There are more people than I think.
Does the reaper's sickle reach*
The furthest star, the best of each?

*Matthew 13:36-43

SKI MASK

It has been said
Do not befriend
    The great.
The higher one is
The harder decisions
    They make;

And at some point
They will disappoint
    And fall,
Having to choose
The lesser of two
    Evils.

Friends of the Most High
Will close their eyes
    At crunch time.
It would be better to die
Or to live a lie
    Than without Him.

For although He allows evil
This is not the devil's
    Hell.
What then of the demons—
Who created them
    So well?

"They must be His sons"*
Let off to run
    And strayed—
Like man has done.
Thus the price of fun
    Is paid:

Reality
Is like gravity—
    You do what it says.
Free Will
Is the Red Pill
    That opens the gates.

These walls all around
Are the walls of a playground.
Some kids push you on the swing,
Others push you down...

*The Apology of Socrates

Holy hands become dirty
Only as He responds
To our own deserving,
Reigning in or loosing
    His hounds.

We can establish the
    Kingdom,
Or establish decay.
It is easy for the Dawn
To make the night go away.

But since we put Him in a
    hard bind
God wears a ski mask.
He's wanting to take it off
And waiting for us to ask.

Good and Evil Angels Fighting for a Newborn Child

BONDAGE OF THE WILL

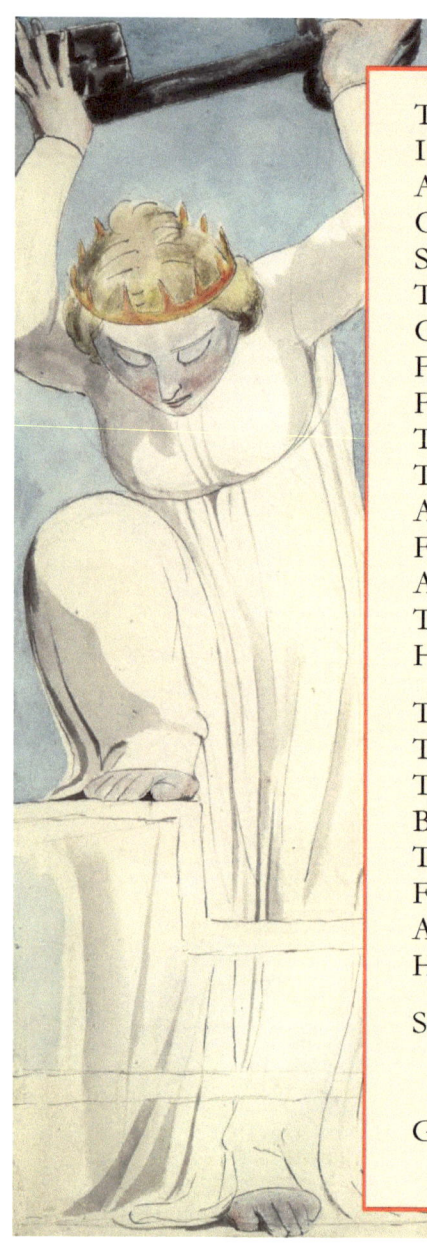

The will is not free
If it has no options;
And if the Maker orchestrates
Our situations
So that we choose good or not,
Though the faculty
Of choosing is present
Fate determines our destiny.
Free Will or Predestination?
They are the same—
Two sides of the same coin,
A means and an end.
For though I could go off
And do some crazy thing,
That just isn't how
He has been training me.

Then we must posit
The existence of miracles—
The movement on the physical
By the spiritual.
This I hardily believe
For I have tested it,
And against all odds
He has manifested.

So why does He choose some,
   and not others?
      Oh brother!
Go read the book of Romans
   from cover to cover.

TO EACH HIS OWN

Each one must laugh his own
    laughs
And cry his own cries.
It is for yourself that you are
Either foolish or wise.
But when I sit in the country
And ponder my blessings,
My heart is so full
I wish that others could see.

THE LITTLE THINGS

It is the little things that count:
A nice sweater for bed;
A fresh loaf of organic multi-grain
     bread.
Unplug the water cooler:
Serve it lukewarm instead;
The kettle and wood screen-door
Sound like music in my head.
Dressed well, with some ornaments
To celebrate the moment,
And all of my needs met,
I am more than content.
Why should I buy into the
     madness—
The opinion of the masses—
That to live happily
It means endless luxury?

"Fools all! who never learned
how much better the half is than the whole."
—Hesiod

There are as many reveries
As there are melodies.

I came into your town
And sang a beautiful song.
Whether I say this or that
You accuse me of wrong.
My wife calls me King;
My children bring me flowers;
And salvation has come to this
    house
This very hour.

Here ends Reveries I

THE AUTHOR

Vincent Orion Aleman is the founder of *Athena Press*, publisher of collectible Classics. Ten percent of all profits are donated to helping rescue the victims of human trafficking. He lives in East Tennessee with his wife and their four children.

William Blake (1757-1827) was an English mystic, poet, and painter in watercolors. Largely unrecognized during his lifetime, he is now included in the poll of BBC's 100 Greatest Britons, and he has been hailed by modern art critics as "far and away the greatest artist Britain has ever produced" (The Guardian).

OTHER BOOKS BY VINCENT

Cardinal Points

Lightning Source UK Ltd.
Milton Keynes UK
UKHW051332280721
387884UK00001B/2